# KILLER !
## SCIENCE

PRESENTS

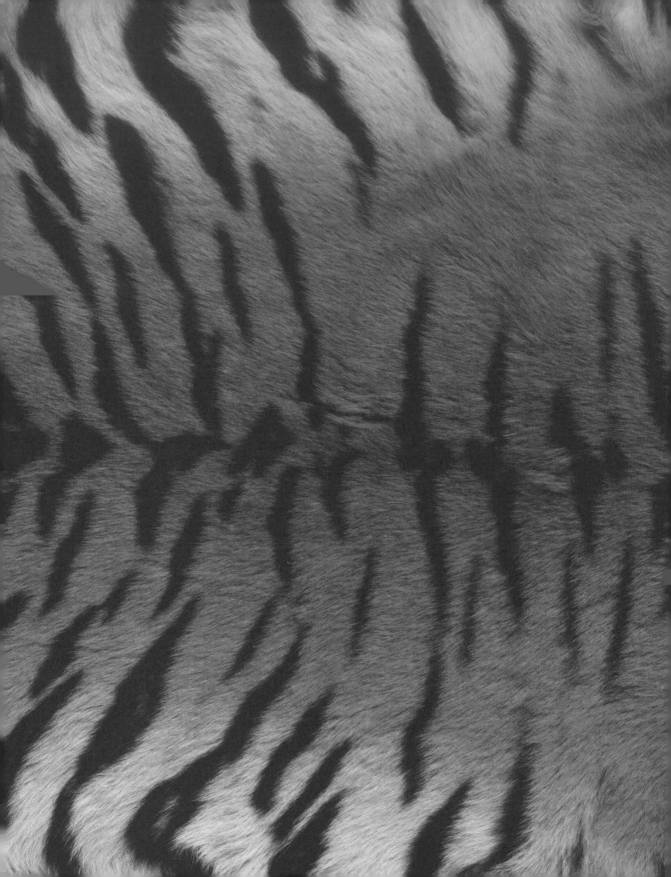

# Nature's Deadliest Predators

## SHELLY SILBERING

ROXBURY PARK

LOWELL HOUSE JUVENILE

LOS ANGELES

NTC/Contemporary Publishing Group

Published by Lowell House
A division of NTC/Contemporary Publishing Group, Inc.
4255 West Touhy Avenue, Lincolnwood (Chicago), Illinois 60646-1975 U.S.A.

Lowell House books can be purchased at special discounts when ordered in bulk for premiums and special sales. Contact Department CS at the following address:

  NTC/Contemporary Publishing Group
  4255 W. Touhy Avenue
  Lincolnwood, IL 60646-1975
  1-800-323-4900

ISBN: 0-7373-0124-4
Library of Congress Catalog Card Number: 99-72109

Roxbury Park is a division of NTC/Contemporary Publishing Group, Inc.

Managing Director and Publisher: Jack Artenstein
Editor in Chief, Roxbury Park Books: Michael Artenstein
Director of Publishing Services: Rena Copperman
Editorial Assistant: Nicole Monastirsky
Interior Illustrations: Jeffrey Domm
Interior Photos: Buddy Mays Travel Stock Photography
Interior Design: Kristi Mathias
Interior Typeset: Bret Perry

Printed and bound in the United States of America
  00 01 RDD 10 9 8 7 6 5 4 3 2

For Mother Nature and our increased understanding of the intricate web of life. And most especially for Bronka, who has survived her own brushes with terror.

—SS

# T A B L E   O F

# CONTENTS

Throughout time, we as people have been at odds with those animals on earth and at sea who are bigger, stronger, and more deadly than we are. We have seen these animals as evil and malicious killers, out to maim and destroy. Nothing strikes fear into our hearts like the open jaws of a white shark (also called a great white shark). Nothing can be as horrific as the thought of being attacked by a grizzly bear while on a camping trip. Being eaten by a tiger is unimaginable to us, but it happens. And the idea of being swallowed by a pointy-toothed alligator makes us shiver in fear. But we are drawn to these stories. Maybe it's because we are ourselves a heartbeat away from such dangers.

Although we often lose sight of the fact that we, as human beings, are mammals, we know we are a part of nature. Just as we "prey" on other animals such as cows, pigs, and fish, other animals may see us as prey. Horrifying, but true. Our population is growing. We are moving into natural areas, destroying forests, prairies, and wetlands. We, as tourists, are even moving into the sea. The animals who call these areas home are the losers. We sometimes lose sight of the fact that nature relies on balance. Disturb one part of nature and a whole environment may be at risk. We are invading their homes and chasing out the other animals who are food to these mighty predators, so we become their prey.

Fortunately, we do have ways to protect ourselves. And fortunately, we do recognize the importance of these magnificent deadly predators. Efforts are underway to protect their natural habitats while also protecting ourselves. With some foresight and a lot of work, with increased effort to keep us all safe from danger, we will be able to read stories of past close encounters with deadly predators and feel our hearts thump, knowing we are safe from danger. And with more foresight, some luck, and a lot of hard work, these magnificent animals, animals who not only kill for a living but also keep herds healthy, fertilize plants, and/or make life-saving water available to many different species, will be around for a long, long time.

## Now, let's find out about nature's deadliest predators!

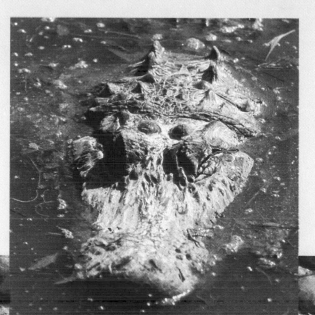

## Shark Attack

What is the scariest thing that could ever happen to you? Some people would say being attacked by a shark is by far the most frightening experience they can think of. The idea is nearly unimaginable. Yet for some reason, we are all curious about what exactly that would be like. What does happen during a shark attack? It goes something like this:

You and your family are on vacation in Australia. You're excited to be so far away from home and in a different country. You've never seen the ocean before, but you're a strong swimmer. You're wearing snorkeling gear and can't believe all the beautiful fishes you're seeing. You forget to pay attention to where the rest of your family is.

Suddenly, something hard bumps into you. Your wind is almost knocked out of your body. Before you know it, you're dragged under the water. You see blood everywhere. It takes a moment for you to realize it's your blood. You don't even feel any pain at first. Not until the monster with the grip on your leg starts to shake you violently. You hear a wild screaming and realize it's your own voice. Your older brother swims out to save you. For reasons unknown to us, sharks rarely attack the person swimming out for the rescue. The shark lurks at a distance as you're dragged back to safety. Later in the hospital you hear that you have a 1-foot-long row

of teeth marks on your leg that are now all stitched up. You have lost a lot of blood, but you'll be okay. The shark must not have been very hungry because your wounds are evidence of a halfhearted shark attack. If the shark meant business and was intent on making a meal of you, its teeth would have easily sunk into your flesh and crushed through the bones of your leg.

It's not likely that any of you will ever be attacked by a shark. Only around a hundred people in the world are attacked by sharks within a one-year period. Most of those people survive. And most kinds of sharks would never even think of attacking a person. Sharks never set out to go hunting for people, but if you're in the path of a shark and if the shark is hungry, you could be dinner!

There are over 375 species of sharks and new species are yet to be discovered. They range from the 7-inch-long dwarf shark to the 60-foot-long whale shark. The many shark species fill a variety of roles in the ocean world. Some live in fairly shallow waters; some live in deep waters. Some eat by attacking their prey; some merely swim with their mouths open, scooping up their dinner as they move along. One reason we fear sharks so much is because scientists have only just begun to study them and learn about their biology, lifestyles, and behaviors. Let's read on to find out what it is we have learned about sharks so far.

**DID YOU KNOW?**

THE WORD SHARK COMES FROM THE GERMAN WORD *SCHURKE,* WHICH MEANS A VILLAIN WHO FEEDS ON OTHER BEINGS.

# From Ancient Times to Now

**A** million years is a long time. We can't even imagine a time period that long. If we took a trip back in time to a hundred years ago we would be able to find our great-great-grandparents. Who would we find a million years ago? Amazingly, sharks have been around for 400 million years! They swam the seas 200 million years before dinosaurs roamed the land. That's long before human beings even existed. Sharks are indeed, like the dinosaurs, prehistoric creatures.

You would think it's no wonder that some people say sharks are primitive animals. The truth is that some sharks have existed for almost 100 million years in their modern form. They've existed for so long because their bodies and behaviors are perfectly matched to their environment. Those shark species that have changed, or evolved, over time have been perfected for life in the waters. Of course there have been species of shark that have become extinct, having been unable to evolve and adapt to the ever-changing environment. Adaptations are continuing even today. So sharks may have existed in primitive times, but they are certainly highly adapted, modern animals who rule the seas.

People didn't know much about sharks until the mid-1900s. It was World War II that brought shark study to the surface of scientific research. Frightening and horrific stories of planes being shot out of the sky and dropping to the sea and of ships being sunk were told over and over again during the World War II. The crew members of these sunken ships and planes were being devoured by sharks.

## DID YOU KNOW?

MILLIONS OF YEARS AGO THERE WAS A SHARK WHO HAD TEETH 7 INCHES LONG! A RULE OF THUMB IS EACH INCH OF SHARK TOOTH EQUALS ABOUT 10 FEET OF SHARK BODY. THAT MEANS THIS SHARK WAS 70 FEET LONG. THAT'S THREE TIMES LONGER THAN THE LARGEST WHITE SHARK FOUND SO FAR!

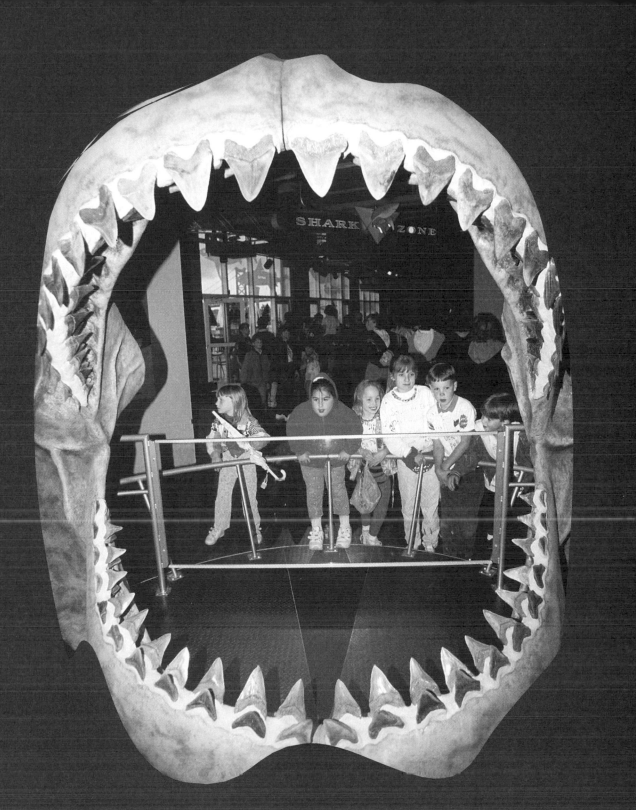

The giant jaws of a prehistoric shark delight children and adults
at the famous Camden, New Jersey , aquarium.

One account of a ship being sunk during World War II tells of 800 men escaping the sinking ship. These men hung onto life for two days when sharks began to show up and circle the escapees. One by one, these men were pulled under the water by the sharks. Four days after the sinking of the ship rescuers appeared. Only a few more than 300 men had survived the wreckage and the shark attacks.

Over and over again, stories such as this one were reported during World War II. Finally, the United States government asked scientists to find out how to prevent sharks from attacking people. These studies still go on today.

Sharks, as I'm sure you know, are fishes. They belong to a class of fish called *Chondrichthyes*. Many physical features distinguish them from other fishes. One of the most distinctive differences is that fish classified as Chondrichthyes have skeletons made of cartilage rather than bone. Chondrichthyes fishes are divided into two subclasses. The *elasmobranchs* is one of the subclasses and is made up of sharks, skates, and rays. Let's take a look at how elasmobranchs differ from other fishes.

## DID YOU KNOW?

**ALL ANIMALS ARE ORGANIZED INTO A SPECIFIC SCIENTIFIC CLASSIFICATION. EACH CLASSIFICATION INCLUDES PHYLUM, CLASS, ORDER, FAMILY, GENUS, AND SPECIES. SCIENTISTS USUALLY IDENTIFY ANIMALS USING THEIR GENUS AND SPECIES NAME.**

Rays and scates such as these are closely related to sharks.

# Anatomy of a Shark

Elasmobranchs have unique characteristics that set them apart from other fishes. First of all, you should know that there aren't major differences between sharks and the skates and rays. Sharks are separate in our minds mainly because skates and rays don't fit the image we have of sharks. But we have to keep in mind that although the typical shark is bullet shaped, there are flat sharks who look strikingly similar to the typical shape of a skate or ray. Let's examine the elasmobranchs.

All elasmobranchs, including the sharks, rays, and skates, have five to seven gill slits. Most elasmobranchs have mouths tucked under their heads and an underslung jaw. And on top of it, an elasmobranch's mouth is filled with rows of teeth that are being continually replaced throughout their lives. They have rough skin made of the same material as their teeth, and a tail fin made of a large top lobe and smaller bottom lobe. Let's dive in and take a closer look at the bodies of these amazing hunters of the sea.

## Touring the Inside of a Shark

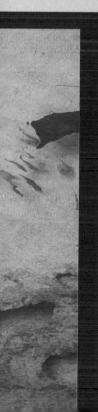

We already know that sharks have cartilage instead of bone making up their skeletons. Mother Nature does nothing without a purpose. So why would cartilage be more advantageous than bone to the well-being of sharks?

Although some shark species do have a bit of bone making up part of their skeleton, cartilage is by far a better material for the shark. The advantage of cartilage is that it is an elastic and flexible tissue that continues growing throughout a shark's life. What does this mean to a shark? It means that the shark's skeleton will not limit the shark's size. The other advantages are that the stretchy cartilage helps sharks move gracefully in the water. And cartilage is lighter than bone, which is a great asset because it helps sharks stay afloat.

DORSAL FIN

OVARY

STOMACH

2ND DORSAL FIN

CAUDAL
FIN

ANAL FIN

INTESTINE

LIVER

PELVIC FIN

ANATOMY O

GILL

NOSTRIL

HEART

CARTILAGE FOR PECTORAL FIN

PECTORAL FIN

GALL BLADDER

F A SHARK

But sharks are fish, so why would they need help swimming? Sharks don't have swim bladders as most bony fishes have. Bony fishes adjust the amount of air in their swim bladders, thus regulating their buoyancy, their ability to float. So why wouldn't sharks have this convenient device? A swim bladder limits the ability of fish to swim through a wide range of water depths. This means that bony fishes, with swim bladders, have a hard time swimming up and down through widely varying depths of the sea, something sharks do all the time. Having a swim bladder may also be a limitation to how large a fish can grow. So besides their lightweight cartilage, do sharks have anything else to help make up for the lack of a swim bladder? Indeed they do.

Sharks rely on accumulating certain oils in their livers to help them stay afloat. Some sharks, such as whale sharks, depend on their oil-laden livers to keep them from actually sinking! And some sharks have livers so large that they make up one-third of their body weight. Slowly, sharks can regulate the amount of oil in their livers, thereby controlling their buoyancy. The oil serves a double purpose. It also provides a shark with much needed energy when there is not enough to eat.

Some sailors believed that sharks could roar. That's not likely to be true. A more likely explanation is that sand tiger sharks, and a few others, gulp in air to help them increase their buoyancy and stay afloat. When fishermen caught these sharks, they may have heard air coming out of the dying sharks' stomachs, making sounds similar to a roar.

We all know that fishes need to breathe oxygen, just like we do. But how do they get oxygen while underwater? Gills. All fishes have gills to help them breathe. Gills take oxygen from the water, acting a bit like our lungs. Most fishes have a gill cover on each side of their heads. They open and close their mouths, continuously sucking water over their gills.

Sharks don't have gill covers. Instead, they have five to seven gill slits on each side of their heads. And sharks don't open and close their mouths to pass water over their gills. Sharks pass water through their gill slits by swimming or by contracting muscles.

Some people believe that all sharks must swim continuously in order to breathe. But how could this be? Types of sharks called bottom dwellers spend most of their time resting motionless on the floor of the sea. Of course they're breathing. They're contracting the muscles between their mouths and throats to pump the water across their gill slits.

## DID YOU KNOW?

**A SWIM BLADDER IS ALSO CALLED AN AIR OR GAS BLADDER. IT IS A LUNGLIKE POUCH THAT IS CONNECTED TO THE DIGESTIVE TRACT OF A FISH.**

Hammerheads, like other sharks, breathe oxygen by passing water through their gill slits.

## The Skin of the Shark

Fish have scales, right? Well sharks go one better; they have placoid scales. Placoid scales, also called denticles, make a shark's skin feel like sandpaper, at best. At worst, people have experienced having their skin torn and bloodied when a shark merely brushed up against them as it swam by. Placoid scales grow from the shark's skin and can be found in parts of the gills and the mouth lining. Even a shark's teeth are placoid scales that have evolved to specialize as crushing and tearing tools.

Placoid scales vary in shape and size depending on the species of shark. These scales were probably an adaptation that helped each type of shark to live efficiently in the sea. How can scales make a difference as to whether a shark lives or dies? The shape of the scales affects the way water flows over a shark's body. This is important to a shark's speed and flexibility. Bottom dwellers, sharks who spend most of their time resting on the ocean floor, don't rely on speed for getting through their day. These sharks have nubby scales, which have no effect on a shark's speed. Those sharks who are superb and fast swimmers have flatter mushroom-shaped scales. These scales also have ridges that face backward, paralleling the water flow, which streamlines the shark for faster swimming.

**Placoid scales vary in shape and size, and they cover most of a shark's body.**

# The Perfect Predator

So what's wrong with being the perfect predator? Look at the food chain in the water and on land. Notice that sharks and humans hold the same position, the top position, as the perfect predator—sharks in the water and humans on land. We humans would probably not warm up to the idea of being called the perfect predator because our "hunting" has been much refined. We now "hunt" at the grocery store. But, indeed, the manifestation of this title is what has allowed sharks to thrive. And thrive they have with a basic body design that has served them well. Some species of sharks have remained practically unchanged for 100 million years.

What goes into being the perfect predator? For humans it has been our mental capacity. For sharks it is primarily the combination of all their senses. Like us, sharks have the five senses of sight, smell, hearing, touch, and taste—but they also have a sixth sense: the ability to sense electrical fields. The actual physiology that makes up the shark's senses is somewhat different from ours. Let's take a look.

## Swimming Noses

Sharks breathe through their gills, leaving their noses free to detect odors. Sharks have a flap that divides each nostril. Water flows into the shark through the outer side of each nostril and out of the shark through the inner side. Inside each nostril is the olfactory organ, which has cells that sense odors. Rather than being smooth, the olfactory organ is made up of folds of tissue that water winds through, allowing it to touch more surface area and therefore more odor-sensing cells. The more of these cells the water touches, the more information that is passed on to the shark.

**DID YOU KNOW?**

THE GREAT WHITE SHARK IS THOUGHT TO BE THE MOST PERFECT OF UNDERWATER PREDATORS. THE FEMALE GREAT WHITE SHARK GROWS 17 TO 21 FEET IN LENGTH AND CAN WEIGH UP TO 7,100 POUNDS! MALES GROW TO A MERE 15 FEET.

Before people ever studied sharks to any degree, we thought that a shark's sense of smell was its most developed sense. We dubbed sharks *swimming noses*. A shark's nose protrudes far in front of its mouth. People used to think that sharks had to roll over onto their sides or backs to take a bite of their prey. Of course they don't. Instead, sharks can dislocate their jaws, sometimes even being able to thrust their jaws in front of their long snouts! Sharks do have a great sense of smell, but as you will see, their other senses are highly developed as well.

### Glowing Eyes

When you swim under water, do you open your eyes to take a look around? If you do, you've probably noticed that life underwater is not as well lit as life on land. In the back of each eye, sharks have a series of plates that reflect light to the front of the eye. These plates are called the *tapetum lucidum* and allow sharks to see better in the underwater conditions of dim light. The tapetum lucidum is responsible for eyes glowing in the dark when light hits them. Some land animals who are more active during the night also have a tapetum lucidum. You've probably seen the glowing eyes of the mysterious cat.

Sharks, like people, have eyes with pupils that dilate under dim light conditions to allow more light to enter. Of course, pupils become slits under bright light conditions. Sharks are able to see in varying light conditions and in waters that are clear or murky.

People who have survived shark attacks and those who fish for sharks exclaim that right before some sharks, such as the great white shark, take a bite, their eyes roll back into their heads, giving the impression that they are blindly lunging for their prey. What's really happening is that the eyes are being covered by nictitating membranes, which are inner eyelids that close from the bottom up. Not all sharks have nictitating membranes. For those who do, the nictitating membrane protects their eyes from being clawed or otherwise damaged while still allowing them to see. Many other animals, again land animals, also are equipped with nictitating membranes. Watch your pet dog or cat's eyes the next time it's taking a nap.

## Hearing and the Lateral Line

You can look a shark over from nose to tail, but you'll never find the shark's ears. Sharks do not have any obvious outer ears, but they do have inner ears. These inner ears are especially equipped to pick up pulsating sounds in the water. How would that help a shark, you may wonder.

Sharks find it easier to catch and eat fish in trouble than to hunt healthy fish. Fish in trouble usually aren't strong fighters or swimmers. Healthy fish swim differently from captured or dying fish, whose jerky and erratic movements signal sharks that easy prey is nearby.

Connected to a shark's inner ear are special organs that form the lateral line. As with ears, there is one lateral line on each side of a shark's body. Although the lateral line plays a role in the shark's sense of hearing, it really is a specialized sense of touch. As fish swim, they make waves or currents in the water. Organs in the lateral line feel the slightest movement of water flowing over a shark's body. The lateral line is another sense organ that tells a shark when food is nearby.

## Taste and the Sixth Sense

So far the shark's senses of smelling, seeing, hearing, and touching have all been described as being well developed and made for hunting. The sense of taste also is important to sharks on the hunt. Sharks have the greatest number of taste buds concentrated right behind their teeth. Taste is the last sense sharks use before deciding to swallow their prey or spit it out. But these five senses aren't the shark's only senses. Sharks have a sixth sense, that of sensing electrical fields.

Many animals of the sea have an electrical field surrounding themselves. Electrical fields are produced through muscle activity and chemical reactions in the animals' bodies. Sharks sense these electrical fields through organs called ampullae of Lorenzini.

Look closely at a shark's head and mouth. You'll see a system of pores. These pores are connected to pouchlike organs called ampullae. Inside each ampulla are five or so nerves that sense electrical fields. Many stories abound of sharks bumping their potential prey before actually taking a bite. These sharks are likely using their ampullae of Lorenzini to get more information from the soon-to-be meal. The ampullae of Lorenzini may be able to tell a shark how strong or healthy the prey is, maybe even if the prey is tasty or not. This sixth sense may even help sharks be precise in their attack.

**DID YOU KNOW?**

A SHARK'S JAWS ARE SO STRONG THAT THEY CAN APPLY AS MUCH AS 18 TONS OF PRESSURE PER SQUARE INCH WHEN THE SHARK BITES ITS PREY!

So there you have it. A hungry shark swims along. It smells a bit of blood. It hears the pulsating sounds of a fish in trouble and feels choppy water currents, further convincing it that prey is close. It swims toward its next meal and sees an injured fish thrashing about. The shark bumps up against its next meal and with precision opens its great mouth and bites the tasty fish. The shark is hungry no more.

But what if there is no injured or dying prey in the waters? Sharks have other "tricks" to add to their repertoire of perfect predator. The great white shark, for instance, has row upon row of serrated, triangular teeth that can be up to 3 inches long. Depending on the species, sharks have from five to fifteen rows of backup teeth ready to be of service. The serrated teeth are perfect for ripping apart the shark's prey. Not all sharks have such formidable teeth, but almost all of them do have rows of teeth. These teeth are loosely attached to a shark's jaw, allowing them to fall out fairly easily. Every time a tooth falls out or wears down, there's another one right behind to take its place! You'll have a hard time finding a toothless shark, no matter how old it is.

Another type of hunting "trick" used by sharks can be found in their coloring. The great white shark, the most perfect of all predators in the sea, usually swims near the surface of the water. Its upper body is dark gray. When seen from above, the shark blends in with the dark color of the water. The bottom half of the great white shark's body is white. When seen from below, this hunter of the seas blends into the light color of the sky. Most sharks have one such trick or another to keep them nearly invisible to their prey. This may be why even people are often taken completely by surprise when they are attacked by sharks.

Why would a shark attack a person? First of all, although sharks have their preferred meals, they don't seem to be picky about what they eat. Horses, boots, and license plates are only a few of the items that have been found in shark stomachs. But some of the great white shark's favorite foods are seals, sea lions, and sea turtles. Think about it. Imagine someone on a surfboard swimming out to catch a wave. How do you think that person looks to a great white shark from underneath? A sea turtle maybe, or a seal? Many reports of people being attacked by sharks also include reports of the shark spitting out or letting go of the hold it had on the person, presumably because the shark wasn't pleased with how the person tasted.

Another factor contributing to sharks attacking people is that more and more of us are invading the shark's territory through recreation areas. We are also polluting the seas more and killing off some of the shark's prey. We are, in some cases, unknowingly serving ourselves up for shark dinner!

Whatever the reason, we must always keep in mind that if we are swimming, boating, or fishing in shark territory, we must respect this most perfect hunter of the seas.

**DID YOU KNOW?**

YOU HAVE A 1 IN 300 MILLION CHANCE OF BEING EATEN BY A SHARK. YOUR CHANCES OF BEING KILLED BY A BEE STING IS 50 TIMES GREATER THAN BEING KILLED BY A SHARK.

# Sharks: Friend or Foe?

**W**here do sharks live? You can pretty much find sharks in any ocean. Some sharks live near shore in shallow waters while others live far from land, deep in the sea. Most sharks live in warmer waters; some even migrate with the seasons. Many sharks start their lives in nurseries. Even though they will live in deep ocean waters when they grow up, they begin life in the shallows, where food is plentiful and easy to find. Let's take a look at the most dangerous of all the sharks.

Only about 20 species of sharks are known to attack people. Out of around 375 species of sharks known to us, 20 is not a large number. A list of the most dangerous sharks would have to include the white shark, the oceanic whitetip shark, the bull shark, the tiger shark, the hammerhead shark, and the blue shark.

## The White Shark

The most famous member of the mackerel shark family is the white shark. Also known as the great white shark and white death, among other names, scientists call this shark *Carcharodon carcharias*. Although other shark species are more deadly to people, the white shark is the most feared.

White sharks are a rare find in the ocean. But they can be found in nearly all warm waters. They swim the Atlantic Ocean from Newfoundland to Florida. They've been sighted in the Gulf of Mexico and in the Pacific Ocean from Mexico to Alaska.

# The Requiem Sharks

A requiem is a song for the dead. The requiem sharks are among the most deadly of all sharks. Some people believe the whitetip shark, known by scientists as *Carcharhinus longimanus* is the most dangerous of all the sharks. This shark lives mainly far from land, though, so it doesn't pose much of a threat to us. But another requiem shark—the bull shark, *Carcharhinus leucas*—is probably the most dangerous of all sharks to human beings. Why? Because there are a lot of bull sharks. They are often seen in shallow waters and they have even been sighted swimming about in freshwater —all likely places for human swimmers to be frolicking.

The bull shark makes its home in the waters off of New York down to Florida and through the Gulf of Mexico. It also is found off the southern coast of California. Bull sharks inhabit the Ganges River in India and the Tigris in Iraq as well. The bull shark has been found as far away from the sea as 1,000 miles, where one was found in the Mississippi River.

Another one of the requiem sharks known to be dangerous to people is the tiger shark, so named because it has markings similar to that of a tiger. Called *Galeocerdo cuvieri* by scientists, tiger sharks are also known as swimming garbage cans by some people. One tiger shark was found with a whole chicken coop in its stomach! Tiger sharks are the most feared shark in the West Indies, where they attack people.

## The Hammerhead Sharks

There are nine different types of hammerhead shark. Most of them are harmless to people. That's not the case with the great hammerhead, *Sphyrna mokarran*.

Hammerheads are the most unusual of all the sharks. An eye and a nostril are at each end of the hammerhead's strangely shaped head. It is thought that the hammerhead is built this way to increase its sensitivity to electrical fields. Having the increased surface area on its head allows for more ampullae of Lorenzini, which detect electrical fields. These deadly sharks swim moving their heads from side to side in an effort to pinpoint odors. Some say the hammerhead's oddly shaped head is the key to its superb hunting skills.

These sharks also can be found in the warm seas of the world. They have been seen swimming in schools, which is an amazing and formidable sight.

That some sharks attack people is not hard to explain when you put all the facts together. Most sharks hunt for their prey and scavenge for morsels to eat. It's not at all unusual for a shark to eat carrion, animals who are already dead. They are opportunists, much like ourselves. They are rulers of the ocean, much like we are rulers of the land. We fear these "man-eaters." But strangely enough, it is we human beings who are the shark's greatest enemy.

Throughout history we have cast sharks in the role of villain so many times that we've lost sight of their good side. Sharks keep the seas clean. They clean the waters of dead and decaying animals, snacking on the weak sea animals and leaving the strong and healthy ones to reproduce. In some cases, they eat things no other animal would even taste. As a part of nature, sharks play an important role in keeping life in the seas balanced.

But for so long people have been ignorant of sharks, and ignorance produces fear. This ignorance and fear coupled with the shark's amazing skills as predator has made the shark perfect for the role of villian.

So we have hunted sharks. We've hunted them and we've hunted them. We kill more than a hundred million sharks every year. What are we hunting them for?

**DID YOU KNOW?**

**THE EYES ON A GREAT HAMMERHEAD CAN BE AS FAR APART FROM EACH OTHER AS 3 FEET!**

In many cases, we want to be one of those people who wins the fight between human and nature. We want to slay the villain. So we're hauling sharks out of the seas to mount them on our walls as trophies. But the truth is that for as long as we've known about sharks, we've found uses for them.

Since ancient times, the people of China, Rome, and Greece have feasted on the meat of sharks. Even today, shark meat is a mainstay in some countries. Some favorite shark meats are dogfish (used to make the British fish-and-chips), blue shark, white shark, and blacktip shark.

## DID YOU KNOW?

**TO RELIEVE THEIR TOOTHACHES, PEOPLE OF ANCIENT GREECE PRESSED BOILED SHARK BRAINS TO THEIR GUMS.**

Sharks are used in other ways besides as food. Their skins are made into accessories such as belts, shoes, and briefcases. Remove the rough placoid scales and sharkskin makes the perfect polishing cloth for finishing wood furniture. And that wonderful and abundant shark liver oil is used in soaps, cosmetics, paints, and even as fuel in some countries. You can find shark liver oil in medicines, too.

Scientists are studying sharks to learn more about their medicinal uses. Many fishes and other beings in the sea are sick or dying animals. These animals, after spending a lifetime swimming in waters polluted by chemicals and other filth, often become ill with viruses and may even have cancerous tumors growing on their bodies. Sharks eat these animals, yet sharks hardly ever get sick. Scientists want to know why. They believe if they can learn more about the shark's immune system and how it keeps sharks disease-free, science can be armed with information that may help people.

Scientists are using different parts of a shark's body to transplant onto people. Shark cartilage is used as a temporary skin graft for burn victims, and corneal transplants from shark to human eyes are being done.

Then on the flip side, peoples such as some Australian aborigines and Native Americans who lived along the coasts have viewed sharks eligious or cultural icons. Sharks have been depicted all around the world in paintings and sculptures. And certainly you're all familiar with how sharks have become a part of our culture. We make movies about sharks, play shark games, and tell stories about sharks. With sharks being such a big part of our culture and history isn't it a shame that we're knowingly and unknowingly starting to wipe them out?

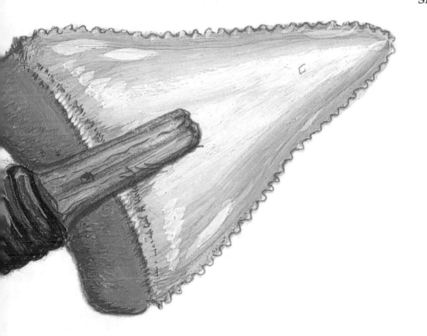

## DID YOU KNOW?

**THROUGHOUT HISTORY, PEOPLE HAVE USED SHARK TEETH AS WEAPONS. THE TEETHS' RAZOR SHARP SERRATED EDGES MAKE GREAT KNIVES AND SPEARS.**

It's not just our hunting that's doing damage to shark populations, but the sheer number of human beings on this earth. We are invading the shark's territory. More and more of us are finding time to take vacations along the world's most beautiful beaches. We're doing more boating, more fishing, more waterskiing, surfing, snorkeling, and more swimming. More and more often, as a shark is swimming around its own neighborhood, it comes upon a human. Why not take a taste? Especially since it's becoming more difficult to find fishes to eat.

Why are fishes and other types of shark food becoming so scarce? We human beings are dumping more pollutants into the seas. Fishes and other sea life are having a more difficult time surviving. The oceans not only are being polluted but they also are going through significant temperature changes. Fishes are sensitive to temperature fluctuations and become sick and even may die. With less to eat, sharks are starting to look elsewhere for their meals.

Although sharks attack around 100 people a year, about 25 of the people die of their wounds. So you tell me who is worse off. The yearly score is sharks 25, and humans 100 million. We win. The shark's future lies in our hands. As we become more concerned about our environment, as we continue to study and develop a better understanding of fearsome beasts such as the shark, we will learn how to coexist with these spectacular creatures.

We have seen how sharks help us in medicine, clothing, stories, and how their beauty and strength inspires us—we have seen how fascinating sharks are. We have learned why sharks attack and how to avoid being attacked. Let's not let our ignorance guide our fears. Let's take our knowledge and overcome the historical battle between human and shark.

**Let's share the earth.**

# GRIZZLY BEARS

# Watch Out for Grizzlies!

Imagine this. You and your family are hiking in the wilderness. Trees and tall grasses fill the landscape. The trail zigzags as it climbs higher up the hillside. There's a slight breeze at your back, cooling you down as you work your way up the trail. It's spring, and everything looks green and fresh. Your whole family is struck by the beauty all around. Each one of you is pointing out this remarkable rock or that amazing plant. You hike around the next bend in the trail and 100 yards ahead of you is a huge bear! A grizzly; you can tell it's a grizzly because of the hump on its shoulders. It stands on its hind legs, sniffing the air. The bear has already spotted you. All that's left for you to see is a blur as the bear lumbers off in the other direction.

Later that day, your family sets up camp. Up goes the tent and up goes the food. The food, stored in bear-tight containers, is hung from a tree high off the ground so grizzlies can't get to it. You eat your sandwiches and settle down for the night. After all that hiking and fresh air, your whole family is exhausted.

Sometime deep in the night you wake up. You hear noises. You smell a rank, sour odor. Bear. All of a sudden your tent is being pushed in. It snaps back with a boing. It's pushed in. It snaps back. The bear is playing with the tent! But then the bear's claws rip through. The rest of your family is awake by now.

Your dad shines a flashlight toward the commotion. Two round, red marbles that are the bear's eyes shine back. The bear lowers its head and charges at you. Your mom and dad start throwing rocks toward the bear and shouting. You clang the metal bowl and spoon you had used earlier for your midnight snack. Was the bear looking for food? Could it smell the trail mix you had eaten from this bowl?

# Bear Country

All Bears Are Dangerous
Use Extreme Caution

Finally the bear turns tail and disappears into the darkness. You and your family don't say a word—you're too stunned and scared. It takes a long time for you to stop shaking. You have just faced death; you were almost attacked by a bear.

Only eight species of bears populate the world. Three of these can be found in North America: the polar bear, black bear, and brown bear. Don't be fooled by these names, though. Although polar bears are almost always white or pale yellow, black and brown bears come in vastly varying colors. Black bears can be light-colored and as brown as some brown bears, and brown bears can be as light-colored as sand or dark enough to look nearly black.

Maybe not the most dangerous bear in North America (that title may go to the polar bear), but certainly the most feared, the brown bear has other confusing aspects to its name. All brown bears are one species. Brown bears around the world are called *Ursus arctos* by scientists. But scientists divide them into subspecies. The brown bears living on islands just off the southwestern coast of Alaska are called *Ursus arctos middendorffi*. Their more common name is Kodiak bear. The grizzly bear is another brown bear subspecies called *Ursus arctos horribilis*.

It's believed by some that the name grizzly comes from the bear's silvery grizzled appearance brought about by the light-colored tips on its long guard hairs. But some people believe the name comes from the grisly mess this bear makes of its prey.

Bears have been worshiped and cursed throughout their long association with people. There are peoples throughout history who believed in the bear spirits. Some of this worship stems from the similarities bears have to humans. It is said that a dead bear when skinned looks remarkably like a human being. And unlike most other animals, who walk on their toes, bears walk flat on their feet more like humans do. And bears can stand!

# History of the Bear

**M**ore than 20 million years ago, an animal much like a small dog roamed the land we now call Europe. This animal, called *Ursavus elmensis*, is considered by most scientists to be the bear's earliest known ancestor. Over the past 20 million years, *Ursavus elmensis* slowly developed, changing form over time into what we now recognize as the modern bear.

Many bear species have existed around the world throughout the past, but today, only eight species of bear roam the earth. Besides the three species of bears already mentioned, the polar, black, and brown bear, five more species of bears exist in the world. The spectacled bear lives in South America while the Asian black bear, giant panda, sloth bear, and sun bear live in Asia. As a matter of fact, the grizzly bear's ancestors are from Asia.

About 1½ million years ago, Asian brown bears lumbered their way from Asia to North America, crossing a strip of land that connected the two continents. This land no longer exists and has been replaced by a passage of water called the Bering Strait. Although brown bears used to live all through the western United States, western Canada, and parts of Mexico, they now are confined to Alaska, small areas of northwestern Montana, and western Canada. What happened to them?

Bears have been cursed. From the moment bear met human, there has been trouble. We both take charge of our environment, so when our paths cross, we compete for space, food, and even the right to exist. Long ago, when the first Americans came face to face with bears, people and bears were evenly matched. The puny, weaker humans had weapons such as stones and bows and arrows. The bears had massiveness, claws, and teeth. These people, Native Americans, respected the bear and lived in balance with nature for the most part.

Then, Europeans began to arrive in North America to colonize the rich land. As they moved westward, they used fast-shooting guns to keep their herds, barnyard animals, and families safe from the mighty grizzly, among other predators. These people hunted the bears for their hides and their meat. But they didn't stop there. Many

**DID YOU KNOW?**

THE POLAR BEAR (ABOVE) EVOLVED FROM THE GRIZZLY BEAR (RIGHT), MAKING THEM THE MOST CLOSELY RELATED OF THE EIGHT SPECIES OF BEAR ALIVE TODAY.

grizzlies were killed by traps and poisons as well as by gunfire. It is estimated that in the 1850s, 100,000 grizzlies lived in the contiguous United States. By around 1900, it is believed that only 1,000 grizzlies remained to roam this land.

As people inhabited more and more of the land, bears were either killed or forced to move to more remote wild lands. Various groups of brown bears were cut off from each other. The Kodiak bears, *Ursus arctos middendorffi*, inhabit Kodiak Island in Alaska and other nearby islands. They tend to be larger than the average brown bear, some weighing over 1,500 pounds! The coastal brown bears live along the coast of British Columbia and Alaska. These bears stuff themselves silly with salmon as the salmon make the difficult trip upstream to their spawning grounds. Coastal brown bears are often called brownies.

The brown bear that has become known as the grizzly bear, *Ursus arctos horribilis*, usually makes its home inland from any coast and is smaller than the coastal brown bear. Let's take a look at what makes a bear a bear.

## DID YOU KNOW?

A GRIZZLY HAS THE STRENGTH TO
TOPPLE A LARGE ANIMAL SUCH AS AN
ELK RIGHT OFF ITS FEET. BUT GRIZZLIES
PREFER TO LEAVE THIS TYPE OF KILLING
TO SOME OTHER ANIMAL. THAT WAY
THEY CAN FEAST OFF A KILL THEY
DIDN'T HAVE TO WORK FOR.

# CHAPTER TWO

# The Bear Statistics

When you close your eyes and think of a grizzly bear, what's the first thing that comes to mind? Is it teeth and claws or fluffy brown fur and a plodding gait? For many people, the distinguishing trait of a grizzly bear is its hump. This hump is formed by huge shoulder muscles that the bear relies on for strength to hunt for food. Bears routinely dig for their meals, push over huge boulders and logs in their quests for a tasty morsel, and use their upper body strength as an advantage when fighting. Of all the bears, only the grizzly has this hump.

Another feature unique to grizzly bears is their dished face. If you look at the profile of a grizzly, you'll notice that the tip of its nose points upward, sometimes leveling off at a point higher than the bear's eyes. If you ever do happen to come across a bear, don't rely on the color of its fur to tip you off to what type of bear you're facing. Instead, look to see if the bear has a dish-shaped face and a hump. If it does, it's a grizzly bear. If it doesn't, then you're probably facing a black bear. Either way, you need to get away from the bear.

Bears have great senses. Their sense of smell is especially keen. The only way you're likely to come upon a bear in the wild is if you're moving quietly downwind from the bear. Usually bears will stay away from human encounters—unless they're surprised. There have been no

reports of people in a group of six or more being injured by a bear, and people in a group of four are rarely injured in bear country. This is truly a case of there being safety in numbers! You, too, can use your sense of smell to tell if a bear is nearby. Bears are known to have a sour odor.

When it's particularly windy, bears are likely to spend the day resting. They get a bit nervous in breezy conditions because the wind tosses odors about, making it difficult for bears to know what's around them.

The bear's senses of smell and sight are enhanced by its ability to stand on its hind feet. If an especially appealing odor wafts by, a bear will stand on its hind feet to get a better whiff. The bear can see farther from this vantage point as well. It's no wonder, too, since a male bear standing on his back legs is surveying the land at a height of about 10 feet!

And what if the bear smells a delicious meal or sees movement in the grass that may mean a ground squirrel is scurrying about? Despite the bear's slow, plodding stroll, bears can speed up to around 35 miles per hour when chasing prey or an enemy. How do you think you would feel if a 500-pound animal were racing toward you at that speed?

To further help a grizzly bear keep tabs on its surroundings are its 4-inch-long claws and 3-inch-long teeth. These sharp claws come in handy when digging for food, tearing bark from trees in search of food, and fighting. The teeth are perfect for crunching through shells and ripping through flesh. But as fierce as bears can be, they are often seen romping and playing, meekly grazing on grasses and flowers, and slowly and peacefully lumbering along, rolling this rock over and peeking under that log for succulent ants. Their formidable canine teeth are sharp enough to tear other animals apart, and their flat molars are perfect for chewing on plants.

Bears are omnivores, meaning they will eat anything. They spend their days fattening up on plants, insects, and meat. Grizzlies dig into burrows, preying on ground squirrels and marmots. They also eat fish and baby mammals such as fawns and moose, elk, and caribou calves. Basically, grizzlies will eat anything they can wrap their lips around. And when summer starts to turn to autumn—watch out! Bears become eating machines. Why? Because they hibernate through most of the winter.

The days get shorter and the temperature drops. Plants die and insects disappear. It's winter. Some animals migrate to warmer climates where they can find food; others store food to dig up throughout the winter. Bears, well they look for a den so they can sleep the winter away.

rizzly bears
an be as
layful
s they are
erocious.

**DID YOU KNOW?**

A BEAR EATS 25 TO 35 POUNDS OF FOOD ON AN AVERAGE DAY. BUT AS WINTER COMES EVER CLOSER, A BEAR GULPS DOWN 75 TO 100 POUNDS OF FOOD A DAY!

39

Grizzly bears dig dens in hillsides or under trees. If they're lucky, they'll find a cave or hollow tree they can call home for a few blustery months. Dens need to be big enough for the bear, but small enough to be warmed up by the bear's body heat. The average size for a den is a surprisingly small 4½ feet wide, 5 feet long, 3½ feet high, with about a 3-foot-long entrance. You would barely fit in a bear den, so imagine the tight fit of a 500-plus-pound bear and maybe even a couple of cubs! For added comfort, bears make beds of evergreen boughs. On warmer winter days, bears make these beds outside their dens.

Bears are not true hibernators. What they do is better described as going into a winter sleep. Some scientists call it carnivore lethargy. A true hibernator's body temperature drops to just above freezing. It takes a few hours for a true hibernator to wake up if it is disturbed during its "sleep." And true hibernators, periodically through the winter, have to wake up, warm up, and go out of their den to "go to the bathroom." So if the bear isn't truly hibernating, then what's going on in the den?

The "sleeping" bear is fully alert. If danger approaches, or for any other reason, a bear can get up right away. Most bear dens are not very deep. That means that wolves and other predators may investigate a den and attack. Since bears go into hibernation at different times from one another, they need to be wary of other bigger bears too. Bear cubs are born in dens, so the mothers must be able to care for their helpless cubs by keeping them warm and fed. Like all mammals, bears nurse their young.

Remember how bears become eating machines as winter approaches? Well, that's because bears live on their stored fat during the lean winter months. Not only does a bear get enough nutrients from its own body, but it makes its own water too. Another amazing feat is that a hibernating bear never has to get up to go "to the bathroom!" Bears' bodies recycle their own wastes. In spring, bears leave their dens a much skinnier version of themselves. On average, hibernating bears lose 25 percent of their body weight.

# DID
# YOU
# KNOW?

BY THE BEGINNING OF WINTER,
BEARS HAVE A 10-INCH
LAYER OF FAT ON
THEIR BODIES.

The bear's den can be a
tight fit for a 500-plus-
pound bear and her cubs.

# CHAPTER THREE

# Predatory Habits

**G**rizzly bears are pretty much the top predator wherever they are. Except when people are around. Even then, though, grizzlies rule unless the people are armed with either weapons or the knowledge of how to avoid a bear attack. The only other exception is for cubs.

Bears have from one to three cubs at a time. Cubs are born in dens during the winter and stay with their mothers for two to three years. Cubs and their mothers need to be on the lookout for wolves and other bears. As a matter of fact, mother bears with cubs underfoot are considered to be one of the most savage animals to encounter. A mother bear will defend her cubs fiercely against any enemy, real or perceived.

Every accomplished predator needs good tools to excel at its job. In most cases, these tools include the animal's senses. We already know that bears have well-developed senses, their greatest sense being their sense of smell. Other tools grizzly bears rely on are their teeth and claws, and their tremendous strength, size, and bursts of speed.

Another tool nearly all predators have is an established territory. Bears, though, are not really territorial. Instead, they roam a home range, which can include hundreds or even thousands of miles, that they often share with other bears. A male grizzly's home range is normally two to four times larger than a female's.

The reason for a bear to stake out a territory or home range is to assure an abundant food supply and adequate shelter. In the bear's case, the home range is its hunting grounds. It includes various areas that have a good food supply at different times of the year. So a bear may go to the northern section of its range in the fall to find a lot of ground squirrels, but stay in the southern range in the spring to gorge itself on grasses and berries. In most cases, bears are happy to share their hunting grounds with other bears.

But like us, and like most other animals for that matter, bears have what some call a comfort zone or personal body space. Each bear has an imaginary circle of space around it. No one is allowed within this space. You have an imaginary circle of space around you. When a stranger stands too close, within your body space, you feel uncomfortable. But if you step within a bear's imaginary circle, you will be attacked.

## DID YOU KNOW?

**EXCEPT DURING THE WINTER, GRIZZLY BEARS HUNT AND REST THROUGHOUT THE DAY AND NIGHT. THEY TEAR OFF TREE BOUGHS OR PILE UP OTHER PLANT MATTER TO MAKE A SOFT, SPONGY BED FOR THEMSELVES. BEARS OFTEN HAVE A NUMBER OF THESE BEDS SPRINKLED THROUGHOUT THEIR AREAS, WHICH THEY VISIT OVER AND OVER AGAIN.**

What are the warning signs? First, especially if you're going to be traveling in bear country, you have to know the difference between an animal being aggressive and one who is acting as a predator. With bears, there is a definite distinction. A bear experiences no anger or stress when it is killing prey. It's important to remember that bears aren't being aggressive when they are hunting—they are being predators.

Think of your pet dog. When your dog catches up with a ball that you've thrown, its ears are up and forward—actually its whole body is leaning forward—its expression is alert, and it looks excited. Chasing a ball may be the closest a pet dog gets to hunting. But when your dog is protecting your house from the mail carrier, its ears are laid back flat on its head, it's leaning back on its haunches, and it's bearing its teeth with a growl. Now that's aggression!

Bears act similar to dogs. A curious bear may approach you slowly with halting steps. Its neck and ears would be craned forward, its nose pointed upward. *Huff huff*, you may hear blowing from the bear's mouth. The bear may be wondering if you're food or enemy.

A hunting bear ready to pounce on its prey will never be angry or stressed. It will look something like your dog chasing a ball. The bear's ears are pointed forward, its eyes are bright with excitement, and its whole body is braced for the kill. An aggressive bear ready to defend itself or its cubs is a different story altogether.

If a bear finds itself in a stressful situation, maybe cornered by a person or trapped, it may yawn and froth at the mouth. A stressed bear looks like it is slobbering. An aggressive bear who is ready to attack sniffs and pants and huffs while circling the object of its aggression. Its ears are laid back flat on its head, and it walks with stiff front legs.

Usually, a bear has to be aggressive when it is faced with another bear. Although most adult bears spend their days alone, bears do have a hierarchy—when two bears meet, one is dominant and the other is subordinate. The dominant bear is usually bigger and stronger than the subordinate bear. Two bears of about the same size hardly ever fight.

If you find yourself face to face with a bear, you're likely to be viewed as the subordinate one. The dominant bear would charge at you, moving stiffly and maybe growling or roaring. Its ears would be laid back flat against its lowered head, and its mouth would be open. You're now facing off with a 500-plus-pound animal who can race you to the nearest tree and beat you to it.

So let's say you really do have a scary bear encounter. What should you do? Play dead. Keep in mind that bears usually swipe at the head when attacking. Lie face down on the ground with your hands crossed behind your neck. Be sure your elbows are tucked in tight against your face and keep your legs slightly apart. Stay in this position for awhile, because even though you can't hear the bear anymore, it still may be watching you.

In a bear-to-bear encounter, the subordinate bear signals that it doesn't want to fight by standing still. Eventually, the dominant bear walks away. The dominant bear is always the one to leave first. So remember, if a bear is approaching you aggressively or not, do not turn tail and run!

Bears attack people for two main reasons. One, because people surprise bears, startling them to defend themselves; and two, because people have food that bears can smell. A bear who enters a person's tent is probably looking for food. The bear is acting as a predator. The safest thing for you to do when hiking in bear country is to make some noise when you're approaching a bend in the trail. Clap your hands or talk loudly. If a bear is in your path, it will get out of your way. If you're camping in bear country, be sure to keep your food out of the bears' reach, out of your tent, and be sure to clean your campgrounds thoroughly before tenting down for the night.

## Never ever feed a bear.

**If you have an encounter with a bear, remember to lie face down on the ground and play dead.**

# Ecology and the Future of Bears

## DID YOU KNOW?

BEAR STANDING UP ON

BACK LEGS LUNGES

RWARD AS IT DROPS TO

L FOURS. MANY PEOPLE

STAKENLY THINK THE

AR IS CHARGING WHEN

EY SEE THIS, BUT IT'S NOT.

E BEAR IS JUST GETTING

CK DOWN

BUSINESS.

**W**hy is it that the grizzly bear has such a reputation for fierceness? People come across black bears, too, but the black bear isn't feared the way grizzlies are feared. It has to do with living conditions.

The black bear lives primarily in the forest. It has trees and other foliage it can use as cover. When threatened, all a black bear has to do is duck behind some trees. Not only that, black bears can climb trees. But brown bears, the grizzlies, generally live in wide-open spaces. There's nowhere to run, no trees to climb. Even if there were trees to climb, only grizzly cubs can actually shimmy up a tree.

In these wide-open areas with no place to hide, grizzlies learned another way to take care of themselves. They learned to fight. And really, what choice did they have? But remember, first and foremost, grizzlies are predators. Their number one concern is finding food and eating.

PEOPLE HAVE KILLED BEARS FOR THEIR MEAT AND FUR AND OUT OF FEAR. BUT WE HAVE KILLED BEARS FOR OTHER REASONS TOO. PEOPLES OF VARYING CULTURES USE BEAR CLAWS AND TEETH AS GOOD-LUCK CHARMS AND BEAR BODY PARTS FOR MEDICINAL PURPOSES.

Over the last hundred years or so, out of fear or for survival, or even for spiritual reasons, people have hunted bears of many types, not just the grizzlies, to near extinction. The human population has grown to such a degree that we're moving into the bear's home. Some bears need hundreds of miles of wild land to survive. But we are now building homes and roads throughout this land.

Grizzly bears are considered a threatened species by the U.S. government. That means so few grizzly bears exist that they are in danger of becoming extinct, or no longer existing. Although people legally and illegally hunt grizzlies, the main threat to grizzly populations is their diminishing habitat.

The government is putting aside protected wildlife areas for grizzlies, but in many cases these are the same areas we vacation at to see, enjoy, and experience nature. It's up to us to be sure that we know how to act in grizzly country so we don't put ourselves or the bears at risk.

## Man-Eaters

The beauty, grace, and stealth of the tiger is nearly unmatched in the natural world. We look at the tiger with awe and respect. To us, the tiger represents unbridled wildness—true nature. Unlike with sharks, grizzlies, and alligators, people don't respond with hate or anger at the mere mention of the tiger or any other wild cat for that matter. Maybe that's because we've invited one of the tiger's relatives, the house cat, into our homes. But more than any other animal, the tiger is associated with the term *man-eater.* Why?

So few tigers exist today that most of us will never encounter one in the wild. Certainly if you live in the United States, you will never see a tiger unless you go to a zoo. But, you may encounter one of the tiger's relatives—the mountain lion.

People have been attacked by mountain lions in the U.S. And although they are truly different species, both tigers and mountain lions use the same methods of attack whether they are hunting other four-legged animals or human beings.

Wild cats attack other animals, including people, with the purpose of killing them and eating them. But if so few tigers exist and if so few people would ever come in contact with a wild tiger, how did the tiger get the reputation of man-eater?

**DID YOU KNOW?**

**MANY MAN-EATING TIGERS HAVE WOUNDS FROM PORCUPINE QUILLS. ONE MAN-EATER HAD 50 QUILLS POKING OUT OF ONE OF HER LEGS!**

## Sneak Attack

*What was that?* You worry as you work out in the field. *Oh, just the grass rustling in the wind.* You're a farm boy in Malaysia finishing your daily chores of checking the cattle out in the field. You're moving fast because you want to get home for dinner. The sun is low on the horizon, so you know you have to hurry; soon it will be dark. *Whap!* You feel your body hit the ground. Stunned, you see the blur of orange and black. A tiger.

The tiger's limping but still strong and ferocious looking. You put your hand up to your face and feel the claw marks the tiger left there. Your hand comes away bloody. Your heart is pounding and you know you can't just lie there. Back on its haunches you can see the tiger preparing to leap. Without even thinking, you roll away from the pounce just in time. You can hear your dad and some of the other villagers running through the field to help you. You hope they'll get to you quickly.

*Bang! Bang! Bang! Bang!* All is still. You hear your dad asking if you're hurt. You feel his gentle touch. You know you are now safe. But when you open your eyes, you can still see that blur of orange and black. You panic, scream, struggle to get away from a grip so strong you can't tell if it's your fear or some other force. Soft words calm you and you realize it's your father's arms holding you close that's keeping you from running. The *bang, bang, bang, bang* wasn't your heart beating but the sound of guns firing. The tiger is dead.

*How could this have happened, you wonder. I'm always so careful, I always look around for dangers. I didn't even see the tiger coming?* Your mind races as you try to figure out how you could have avoided this attack. Finally at home, you sit down to a cool, delicious dinner and the safety of your family.

**DID YOU KNOW?**

MOST TIGERS WHO ATTACK PEOPLE HAVE BEEN INJURED AND ARE UNABLE TO HUNT THEIR NORMAL PREY.

# CHAPTER ONE

# The Tiger's History

It's no surprise to anyone that tigers are members of the cat family. As a matter of fact, nearly every feature of the tiger can be seen in miniature form in the house cat. If you share your life with a cat, you may want to keep tabs on the similarities and differences found between the tiger and your kitty. It's also no surprise to anyone that tigers are carnivores, being one of the most perfect hunters and meat eaters on land. But it may surprise you to know that five types of tigers exist today.

The tiger is a species of animal scientists call *Panthera tigris*. The tiger is further divided into five suspecies. These tigers live in different parts of Asia. The five types of tiger are Indian tigers (*Panthera tigris tigris*), Siberian tigers (*Panthera tigris altaica*), Chinese tigers (*Panthera tigris amoyensis*), Indochinese tigers (*Panthera tigris corbetti*), and Sumatran tigers (*Panthera tigris sumatrae*).

Cats are divided into three categories: The small cats include your pet cat, among others; the cheetahs are in a category all to themselves; and the big cats include lions and tigers, among others. Tigers are the largest of all the big cats. The tigers living farther north tend to be larger than those living in the southern regions. The largest tiger is the Siberian tiger, weighing up to 600 pounds and measuring about 15 feet long.

## Tigers and People

Throughout history, those people who have shared their regions with tigers have incorporated tigers into their lives, one way or another. The tiger is considered both good and evil, and is both respected and hated, depending on the culture. This makes a lot of sense when you consider how tigers can affect these people's lives.

Most people who live near tigers are farmers whose villages were built up near forested areas that tigers call home. Tigers kill and eat animals who are considered pests by farmers. Deer, monkeys, and wild pigs raid crops. When tigers are near, these animals aren't as much of a problem. So tigers are good to have around—they are respected for being great killing machines. But tigers can kill people, so they are feared for being great killing machines.

Many of the peoples of Asia have incorporated tigers into their religions and belief systems. For example, the god Shiva in the Hindu religion wears a tiger skin and rides a tiger to fulfill his role as the destroyer. But the followers of the Buddhist religion believe in gods who ride tigers as a show of their supernatural ability to overcome evil.

**DID YOU KNOW?**

**SOME EXPERTS ESTIMATE THAT FROM THE MID-1500s TO THE MID-1900s, A 400-YEAR SPAN, TIGERS KILLED AROUND 1 MILLION PEOPLE.**

The Chinese even use tiger parts in their traditional medicine, with individual parts curing specific ailments. For instance, tiger claws are used to help people sleep and tiger teeth can treat a fever. Tiger bone can be made into pills to help arthritis and headaches, among other ailments, and tails can treat skin diseases. Whiskers can treat toothaches and tiger brains treat laziness and acne. Tiger feces cure, among other things, alcoholism—that's enough to make anyone say no to drugs! But today, those who practice traditional Chinese medicine have other natural alternatives to the tiger.

Although killing and selling tiger parts is against the law in most countries, still poachers kill tigers illegally. It is estimated that a killed tiger whose parts are used for medicine can be sold for over $20,000!

Now that we have a sense of how people have viewed the tiger throughout history, let's take a close-up look at the animal, the real tiger.

# The Tiger, Stripe by Stripe

The tiger is the largest and most powerful member of the cat family. Yes, the tiger is even more powerful and fearsome than the lion. But take the fur off both creatures and you end up with two animals who are built virtually the same.

More than fur, though, distinguishes the tiger from the lion. For instance, social structure is quite different among the two species. Tigers are almost always solitary, spending their days alone. Lions, especially the females, usually live in groups called prides. The solitary tiger has only itself to depend on for food, safety, and shelter. The tiger had to develop the most perfect hunting technique because it hunts alone.

Tigers hunt with stealth. The key to being a successful hunter is surprise. Tigers have to learn how to be stealthy—how to sneak up on an animal and launch a surprise attack—because tigers cannot run fast for very long. Most of the animals they prey on are great runners. Tigers hardly ever prey on healthy animals because they know that they are not likely to catch them. Tigers usually kill the old, the young, or the injured animals. But even as one of the most accomplished hunters, the tiger misses its kill about 9 out of every 10 times.

The tiger has two main methods of killing. One is to use its powerful front paws to knock the prey animal off its feet and then pounce on the animal. The other method is to use its jaws to seize the prey immediately by the back of the neck or throat. Either way, the tiger kills the animal by breaking its neck or by squeezing its throat until it suffocates.

What are the tools of such a powerful hunter? Well, they're all built into the tiger, and they all work together to ensure the predator's success. Let's start with the most obvious—the fur.

the tiger. But it is exactly the flashy orange with black stripes that keep tigers hidden in the tall grasses and trees of the regions that tigers call home. The stripes actually mingle with the patches of sunlight that stream through the shadows cast by the foliage surrounding a tiger. The tiger's seemingly bright coloration is exactly what camouflages it in its natural habitat. Each tiger has a different and unique stripe pattern.

Tigers must remain hidden so they can sneak up on their prey slowly and silently. To help them with their sneak attacks, tigers have soft pads on the bottoms of their large paws. Some people have even nicknamed the tiger *jungle ghost*, believing there to be a silent white tiger who haunts the jungles.

The tiger's soft, padded, large paws are a bit deceiving. Hidden in individual sheaths in each of a tiger's paws are five long, sharp, hooked claws that can be used as weapons to wound prey. Claws come out of their sheaths at the tiger's will—when the tiger is ready to attack, to help the tiger eat, and sometimes to mark territory. Claws are also used to grip onto moving prey while the tiger delivers the final deadly bite.

The tiger's jaws and teeth are important hunting tools. Powerful jaws can exert enough pressure to break the neck of a large hoofed animal who may weigh as much or quite a bit more than the tiger. Tigers have been known to bring down prey weighing over 2,000 pounds!

Tigers are usually about 30 to 60 feet away from their prey before they launch their attacks. They wait to rush out of hiding until the prey animal realizes there's danger and tries to escape. When tigers are hunting large prey such as deer, buffalo, and wild pigs, these neck-breaking, throat-squeezing attacks are made successful by using the prey's own movements. A tiger follows its prey's struggles, using the animal's energy to help tighten the death grip the tiger has on the prey.

The tiger's long, sharp canine teeth are used to puncture its prey's throat. The tiger also has specialized molars in the back of its mouth. Molars are used by many animals, including us, for chewing food. A tiger's molars, called carnassials, are sharp teeth used like scissors to cut food. Tigers can't chew their food because their jaws can't move well from side to side. Instead, tigers swallow chunks of meat and bone, which are processed by strong juices in their stomachs.

Of course, keen senses accompany the tiger's precise skills and built-in deadly weapons such as claws, teeth, and strength. The tiger's vision is highly developed, being able to hunt in the low light conditions of dusk and dawn as well as during the day. Tigers, like house cats, can see well in dim light conditions. They have a tapetum lucidum in the back of each eye. The tapetum lucidum is a series of plates that reflect light to the front of the eye, allowing tigers and all cats to see better when light conditions are low. The tapetum lucidum is also responsible for a cat's eyes glowing in the dark. But the tiger's senses of hearing and smell are highly developed too.

The tiger's senses, well-muscled body, paws, striped fur, teeth, and claws all work together to make the tiger one of the most accomplished hunters in nature. But each tiger also must rely on its experience and knowledge of prey animals and the land.

# King of the Hunters

Tiger cubs stay with their mothers for about two years. As cubs, tigers spend their days practicing the hunt. Sure they may start by stalking a spider or their sister's tail, but all their clumsy efforts as babies help them learn. Their mothers teach them too. At first, when cubs are very young, their mothers hide them when going off to the hunt. But after a while, the cubs go along to watch and learn. Eventually, when the cubs are close to a year old, Mom will bring down an animal, and the cubs will finish the kill.

The only time tigers hunt in a group is when tigers are cubs. A tigress, a female tiger, and her cubs will hunt together for a while, but normally tigers hunt alone. Tigers hunt within an area they've staked out as their territory. A tiger's territory may overlap with other tigers, but even so, tigers usually stay away from one another.

Every now and again, tigers do meet up with other tigers. This often happens over a kill. If food is scarce, a tiger will fiercely defend its kill, keeping all other tigers from eating. The exception is that a tigress shares food with her cubs. But if food is plentiful in the area, tigers are willing to share their kills with other tigers. But the dinner guest doesn't just dig in. He politely waits his turn.

Feasting does not begin immediately after a tiger has successfully killed its prey. Instead, the tiger drags its prey into hiding, usually into long grasses or a thick of trees. There, the tiger starts eating its meal. Usually, dinner starts at the prey's rump. It may take several days for a single tiger to finish eating a large animal. Sometimes a tiger roars to announce its kill and its willingness to share a meal. Sometimes another tiger comes along and steals the kill.

A tiger's claws help tear meat from an animal's carcass, but so does its tongue. How could a tongue be so powerful, you may wonder. Just imagine a house cat. If you've ever been licked by a house cat, you know that its tongue is rough. A house cat weighs on the average about 10 pounds. A tiger weighs about 300 pounds (although weights vary greatly depending on subspecies, diet, and gender). Imagine what a 300-pound animal's rough tongue would feel like on your finger.

Tigers' tongues are so rough that if you were licked by a tiger, your skin would be scraped right off your bones! All cats have papillae, which are spiny protrusions, on their tongues. The papillae are so pronounced on a tiger's tongue that they're used to scrape meat off the bones of prey.

The papillae also help cats, including tigers, drink. Cats use their tongues to collect water, which is normally what cats drink. The liquid collects in the grooves between the spiny protrusions, so when the cat draws its tongue back into its mouth, water is carried along. And all cats use their rough tongues to help them with their grooming chores. The papillae work like combs to smooth and clean fur.

Only a few thousand tigers live in the wild today. That's not very many. Sure, zoos are keeping many of the tiger subspecies alive, maintaining breeding programs and exhibits that are as close to a tiger's natural living conditions as possible. The major reason for there being so few tigers in the world is their diminishing habitat, or land that they call home. Let's take a look at the tiger's home and find out what tigers need to stay alive and how we human beings have affected them.

**TIGERS HAVE BEEN KNOWN TO EAT UP TO 60 POUNDS OF MEAT IN ONE SITTING. ONE TIGER WAS FOUND WITH 100 POUNDS OF MEAT IN ITS STOMACH!**

## Home Alone

**O**ne thing we know for sure is that tigers adapt easily to a variety of living conditions. This means, for instance, that tigers can live in cold areas where the temperature drops to nearly 50 degrees below 0 Fahrenheit, and they can live in regions that become very hot. They can adapt to varying prey, killing and eating small animals such as fish and monkeys or large animals such as buffalo and deer.

Tigers seem to have only three requirements to live: a water supply, hiding places such as tall grasses or trees, and enough animals to eat. They don't care whether they live in swamps or evergreen forests, up high on sloping hills or on flat land. What tigers need is a territory, an area much like a neighborhood that includes a body of water, a lot of prey animals, and hiding places. They also need one or two tigers nearby so they can mate and have cubs.

Most scientists agree that tigers developed in the north, where the temperatures tend to be cool. Of course, they made their way to warm southern regions, which is one reason bodies of water are so important to them. Lions seem to love to bask in the sun during the heat of the day, but tigers prefer to spend the midday hours with most of their bodies under water. Tigers have a funny way of getting into the water. They walk in backwards!

Hiding places in the form of grasses and trees are also essential to a tiger's territory. Tiger stripes work with the foliage and sunlight and shadows to keep a tiger

## DID YOU KNOW?

UNLIKE MOST HOUSE CATS, TIGERS LOVE TO SWIM. THEY LEARN TO LOVE THE WATER AS CUBS. SOME TIGERS WHO LIVE ON ISLANDS SWIM FROM ONE ISLAND TO ANOTHER. DURING THE HEAT OF THE DAY, TIGERS CAN BE FOUND LOLLING IN A BODY OF WATER TO KEEP COOL.

camouflaged. Tigers need to hide for a couple of reasons. They lurk hidden in vegetation to help them launch successful attacks on their prey, for one. And tiger cubs hide from potential dangers in the form of other predators such as leopards and even other tigers. Tiger cubs have just a 50 percent chance of surviving to their second year.

And finally, a tiger's territory must have much more than enough prey for the tiger. It must have an overabundance of prey animals. The population of suitable prey determines how many tigers will share a territory. Remember, a tiger will miss 9 out of 10 times they try to kill an animal. Hunting is difficult. If there weren't a large population of prey animals, it would be much more difficult for a tiger to hunt successfully.

Territory to a tiger doesn't have exact borders that remain the same throughout the tiger's life. The borders vary, sometimes seasonally, sometimes because of an addition or depletion of the territory's tiger population. You see, tigers generally share territories, or a tiger's territory will overlap another tiger's territory. For example, a female tiger's territory in Nepal may cover around 8 square miles, while a male's territory may extend up to 40 square miles.

A female tiger's idea of territory is quite different from a male's. A female usually holds a territory with just enough food for herself and her cubs. A male's territory, on the other hand, is usually big enough to overlap the territories of a few females.

That way, he can father many cubs. It's not ofte[n] though, that more than one tiger is in the same are[a]. But when two female tigers meet, they're often friend[ly] to each other. They may rub against each other and purr.

Tigers have developed a way to let each other know who ha[s] control over a territory. It has to do with scent. Tigers us[e] their urine and feces as messages, which are posted [in] strategic places around the borders of the tiger's territor[y]. The messages let other tigers know the age and gender of th[e] tiger who left them and when the tiger passed through th[e] area. A tiger patrols the boundaries of its territory, leavin[g] such messages over and over again. When another tig[er] comes around, it uses its Jacobson's organ to help "read" t[he] messages. The tiger sniffs the targeted area and perform[s] *flehmen*, a screwing up of the face. Well, that's what it loo[ks] like to us. Actually, the tiger is sucking the scent throug[h] two specialized holes in the roof of its mouth. The scent [is] interpreted by the Jacobson's organ. Your house cat uses [a] Jacobson's organ too.

Tigers also use the scent glands in their cheeks b[y] rubbing their faces against trees and rocks to ma[rk] territory. They leave visual messages as well. Tigers u[se] their claws to leave deep scratches on tree trunks and t[he] ground. Roaming tigers know to stay away when they s[ee] another tiger's claw marks or smell the markings of a[n] established tiger.

Maintaining a territory is a way for tigers to keep pea[ce] among themselves. Sure, fights among tigers do break o[ut]

but every tiger knows that an all-out fight is likely to lead to injuries and possibly death for one or both of the tigers. So it is in every tiger's best interest to keep the peace.

Tigers are loners, and they are killers. Their time is spent primarily resting and hunting. Many attempts at killing prey are needed before a tiger is successful and able to eat. So a tiger needs a lot of land with a huge population of eatable prey.

Over time, we humans have been moving into the tiger's territories. We don't recognize the tiger's scent marking and stay away like another tiger would. We have guns and bulldozers and are able to construct buildings and create farmland in areas once occupied by tigers. The tiger's prey have died off because they don't have the land or the food to survive. The tiger has become hungry—possibly injured and weak as well. As a tiger's habitat and prey dwindle, the tiger becomes more likely to turn to people to prey upon.

So the next time you hear about a man-eating tiger, you'll know that the tiger has probably tried to hunt its regular prey. You can figure that the tiger has become weak with hunger and probably injured by its attempts at hunting smaller prey such as porcupines. You'll know that there have probably already been accounts of a tiger raiding a farmer's herd of cattle. And then you may hear tell of a tiger who has devoured one person after another.

With people building on tiger territory, chasing away wildlife, only around 7,000 tigers now exist in the wild. Of those 7,000, around 3,500 to 4,000 are Indian, or Bengal, tigers. Governments are starting to put aside parcels of land to keep the wild tiger population alive. And although everyone agrees that a tiger who becomes a man-eater must be killed, most of us also agree that it is important to preserve the existence of the largest members of the cat family. Our world surely will be a less-colorful place without the brilliant orange-and-black-striped animal who can quietly disappear into the thicket.

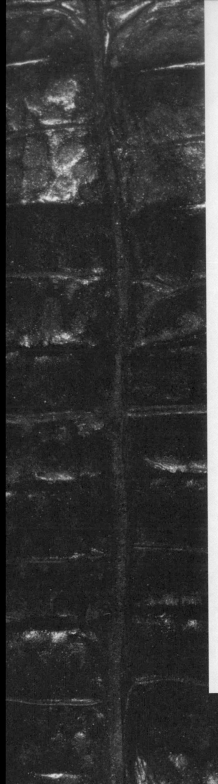

## Mass Attack

It's February 19, 1945. World War II is being fought. Nearly 1,000 Japanese soldiers are making their escape from British soldiers. They are trudging through a mangrove swamp off the coast of what was then called Burma in Southeast Asia. Darkness surrounds the Japanese soldiers and brings with it a most unimaginable danger: Crocodiles.

Rifle shots ring out here and there in the blackness of night. But it's the horrifying sounds of screaming men that fill the ears of the British forces on the outskirts of the swamp. All through the night, men are being crushed by the deadly jaws of enormous crocodiles—reptiles who probably measure over 10 feet long. It is said that the noise was deafening and the scene was much worse than any horror movie. As the sun rose the following morning, only 20 or so Japanese soldiers were found alive. This was by far the worst, most grisly attack by crocodilians ever recorded.

Of all the crocodilians, the Nile and the Indopacific crocodiles are by far the most deadly to people. Even so, most human deaths blamed on these huge, deadly crocodilians happened long ago. Peoples of parts of Africa and Australia tell of fishermen, women washing clothes, and people bathing in bodies of water inhabited by crocodiles losing their lives to be a meal for these deadly predators.

But you don't have to worry—at least not much. Neither the Nile nor the Indopacific crocodiles live in North America. The American alligator and the American crocodile are the only crocodilians living in North America, and even they stay in the southern regions of the United States. The American alligator lives in eastern North and South Carolina; southern Georgia, Alabama, Mississippi, Arkansas; eastern Texas; and in Louisiana and Florida. The American crocodile can be found from northern South America to southern Florida.

The American alligator is much less likely to attack a person than is the Nile or Indopacific crocodile, but alligators can and do attack people. In Florida, an average of six people a year suffer attacks by alligators. But only a small percentage of those people actually die from their wounds. Nevertheless, if you find yourself anywhere near an alligator or crocodile, assume you will be attacked.

**DID YOU KNOW?**

**CROCODILIANS ARE LARGE REPTILES THAT INCLUDE CROCODILES, ALLIGATORS, CAIMANS, AND GHARIALS.**

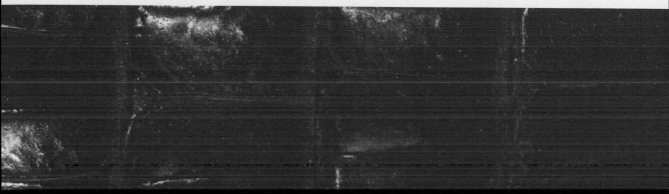

# Living Dinosaurs

The history of crocodilians goes back more than 200 million years. But they are not prehistoric leftovers or simple animals who have somehow survived from a bygone time. Instead, they are highly specialized creatures who have gone through many changes during their 200-million-year history.

If you were to guess what type of animal is most closely related to the crocodilian, what would you guess? If you guessed the lizards, you're wrong. Believe it or not, the closest relatives to crocodilians are birds! Crocodilians and birds share a number of similarities in the structures of their muscles and skeletons. They also both build nests out of plant material, lay eggs with hard shells, and care for their young to some degree. Of course, crocodilians are reptiles. Their second closest relatives are the scaly lizards. Reptiles are animals who crawl on their bellies or walk on short legs. Their bodies are usually covered with scales. Snakes, turtles, lizards, alligators, and crocodiles are all reptiles.

Sometime 65 to 35 million years ago, the alligator and crocodile's ancestors lived throughout Europe and North America. Then the average temperature of the earth changed, cooling to the point where these reptiles could no longer live in their northern regions.

**DID YOU KNOW?**

CROCODILIANS ARE THE ONLY SURVIVORS OF A GROUP OF ANIMALS THAT INCLUDED THE DINOSAURS, WHICH ARE CALLED THE ARCHOSAURS.

## People and Crocodilians in History

Throughout history, many peoples included crocodiles and alligators in their cultures and rituals. Crocodiles were worshiped by some peoples and hated and hunted by others. They were mummified by the ancient Egyptians. Alligators, not being as numerous as crocodiles, were included in the literature of China.

Besides being incorporated into various religions, many myths, stories, and art of ancient peoples include crocodiles and alligators. Many people believe that the Chinese image of dragons is based at least partially on crocodilians. Europeans exploring what is now the United States would return home with tales of seeing dragonlike creatures roaring loudly with clouds of smoke pouring from their nostrils. They were actually describing alligators and crocodiles, none of whom can spit smoke out of their bodies. But alligators looked so much like the Chinese image of a dragon that the truth got a bit twisted.

Tales, religious rituals, and art helped people make sense of animals who were quite different and much more dangerous than most animals of the people's day-to-day lives. In many cases, stories were used to help people understand creatures who were so unusual and so powerful. The rituals were used to keep the animal gods satisfied so no harm would be done to the human population.

During those ancient times, more crocodile and alligator species existed. Today we can find 22 species, or kinds, of crocodile but just two species of alligator. Let's read on to find out how to tell the difference between an alligator and a crocodile.

**DID YOU KNOW?**

BETWEEN 145 AND 65 MILLION YEARS AGO, A HUGE CROCODILE WALKED THE EARTH. IT COULD GROW TO BE 36 FEET LONG! IT'S JAW ALONE WAS 6 FEET LONG, WHICH IS ABOUT THE HEIGHT OF AN AVERAGE MAN. CALLED *DEINOSUCHUS* BY SCIENTISTS, ITS COMMON NAME IS TERROR CROCODILE.

# CHAPTER TWO

# Crocodilians from Head to Tail

The first things you notice about a crocodilian is that it is long, short to the ground, covered with a tough-looking skin, and has a long mouth with a lot of pointy teeth. More likely than not, the animal is near a body of water. As a matter of fact, you may not even know at first that there are any crocodilians around. That's because they spend much of their time underwater. Their nostrils and eyes poke out of the water, while the rest of their bodies are submerged. But crocodilians avoid being in water when there are strong winds and the water is choppy. Since they keep their nostrils above water when they swim, they have problems breathing when there are waves.

The body structures and lifestyles of all crocodilians are similar. They vary mainly in size, head shape, and coloration. The crocodilian's body is made to be in the water. Its long, strong tail uses S-shaped movements to propel the crocodilian through the water, while its legs are kept close to its body. The front feet each have five toes. The back feet each have four toes. The outer toe of each back foot is used to feel things and the three inner toes are equipped with claws. All the toes are partially webbed.

**LARGE AMERICAN ALLIGATORS ARE COMMONLY SEEN IN THE SWAMPS OF THE MISSISSIPPI RIVER IN SOUTHERN LOUISIANA.**

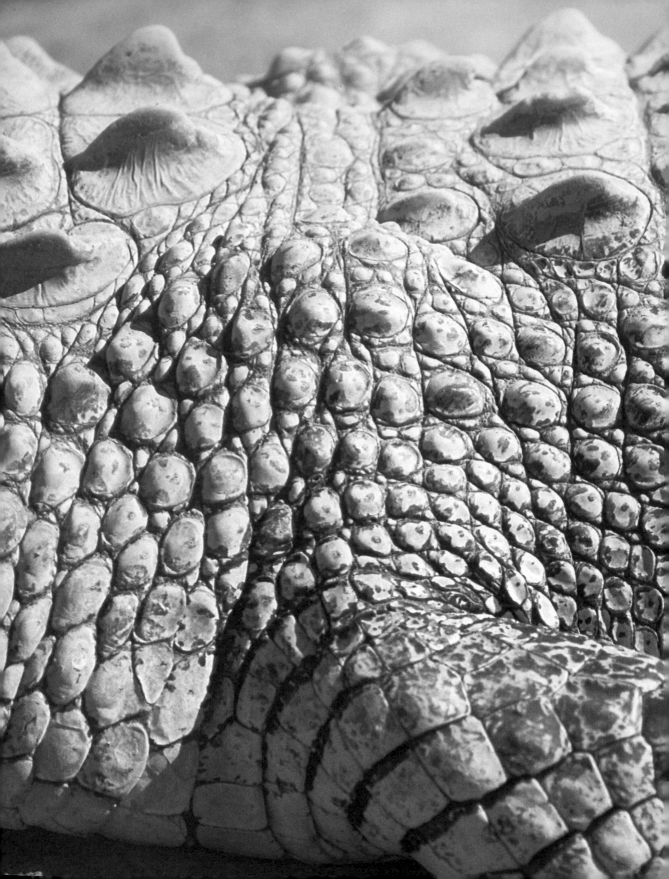

The crocodilian's tough, thick skin is important to its survival. The skin is made of flat, leathery scales called scutes. The scutes are made of the same material that makes up your fingernails. The scales along a crocodilians back contain bone and are thicker and often ridged, giving the crocodilian a dragonlike appearance. The skin is so strong and impenetrable it acts like an armor, protecting the animal from the fierce bites of other crocodilians. The skin on the belly, however, is softer and smoother.

Besides being great swimmers, crocodilians get along on land rather well. They have a variety of ways of walking. Like most other reptiles, crocodilians can crawl on their bellies. But unlike other reptiles, crocodilians also have what is called the high walk.

Some reptiles such as turtles have legs that come out from their sides, lifting them from the ground and allowing them to move in a sprawling sort of walk. Crocodilians, however, can walk more like mammals do. Their legs can be held almost vertically beneath their bodies. This high walk allows crocodilians to move across land at a speed of 0.2 to 3 miles per hour. Some crocodilian species move faster and faster until they end up in an awkward sort of gallop, bounding at speeds from 2 to 10 miles per hour!. The gallop usually ends up with the crocodilian flopping on its belly, twisting from side to side in its effort to move quickly.

Crocodilians cannot move quickly, sometimes not at all, when the temperature drops. That's because they're cold-blooded. It's not really that their blood is cold, it's just that crocodilians cannot control their body temperature from within their bodies. Because the term *cold-blooded* is a bit misleading, scientists prefer to call these animals *poikilothermic*.

Poikilothermic animals cannot shiver to get warm; they don't have fur, feathers, or a layer of fat to insulate them against the cold or to hold heat in their bodies. Instead, the body temperature of poikilothermic animals, such as

the crocodilians, is determined by the temperature of their surroundings. A crocodilian who wants to warm up comes out of the water and lies on the bank, soaking up the warmth from the sun. The crocodilian's dark color helps the skin absorb heat from the sun. Too hot? Well, then the crocodilian can slip back into the cooler water.

During the day, crocodilians spend a lot of their time basking in the sun. Their dark skin absorbs the heat, warming their bodies so they can be active. Often crocodilians bask with their jaws gaping wide open. This may be a way for them to keep their heads cool, and some scientists believe that gaping dries up algae that may have collected in the animal's mouth.

There are certainly pros and cons for an animal to be poikilothermic. The main disadvantage is that when the temperatures drop, poikilothermic animals can't move—they become helpless, unable to search for food, defend their territories, or merely run away from dangers. It takes a while for larger poikilothermic animals such as the crocodilians to warm up and get moving again.

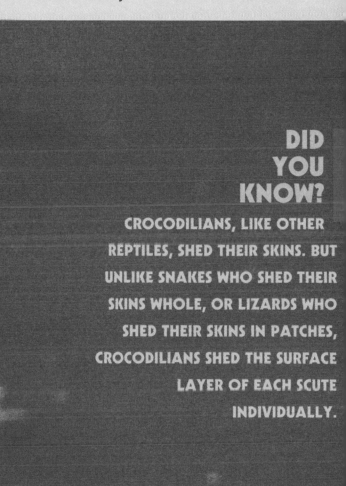

**DID YOU KNOW?**

CROCODILIANS, LIKE OTHER REPTILES, SHED THEIR SKINS. BUT UNLIKE SNAKES WHO SHED THEIR SKINS WHOLE, OR LIZARDS WHO SHED THEIR SKINS IN PATCHES, CROCODILIANS SHED THE SURFACE LAYER OF EACH SCUTE INDIVIDUALLY.

**AN ALLIGATOR BASKS IN THE SUN.**

**SOME ALLIGATORS DO LIVE IN AREAS WHERE THE TEMPERATURE DROPS TO BELOW FREEZING. THE ALLIGATORS MERELY POSITION THEMSELVES IN SHALLOW WATER SO THAT THEIR NOSTRILS KEEP A SMALL BREATHING HOLE OPEN IN THE ICE. IF THE WATER IS DEEP ENOUGH AND THE ANIMAL LONG ENOUGH, THE LOWER PART OF ITS BODY MAY BE IN DEEPER, WARMER WATERS. IT'S NOT UNHEARD OF FOR AN ALLIGATOR TO BE STUCK IN PLACE BECAUSE ITS SNOUT IS FROZEN IN THE ICE!**

The advantage of being poikilothermic is the ability to go without food for long stretches of time. Reptiles, unlike mammals, don't need the additional energy that food provides to keep their bodies warm. Alligators have been known to last half a year without eating any food!

And now for the big question: How can you tell the difference between an alligator and a crocodile? Look at the snouts. The alligator has a flatter and shorter snout than does the crocodile. When their mouths are closed, the lower teeth are visible only on the crocodile. On the lower jaw, the crocodile's fourth tooth, its largest tooth, fits in a notch on its upper jaw. If you look at a crocodile from above, you can see this tooth, one on either side of its head. These teeth give the impression that the animal is smiling.

Crocodilian teeth are made for puncturing and tearing meat. Depending on its size, a crocodilian eats a variety of animals. Smaller and younger crocodilians eat insects, spiders, snails, small fish, and frogs. Larger crocodilians eat larger fish, birds, reptiles, and mammals. Although they spend much of their time in the water, crocodilians successfully hunt land animals as well. Now let's take a look at why the crocodilians earned the reputation of being fierce predators.

**RIGHT: AN AMERICAN ALLIGATOR IN THE WETLANDS OF EVERGLADES NATIONAL PARK**

# CHAPTER THREE

## The Laziest Deadly Animal

Like all good predators, crocodilians must have highly developed tools of the trade. One look at an alligator or crocodile is all you need to know that you never want to get between those prickly jaws! Yes, of course, the teeth are ominous. Their pointy tips pierce flesh so that all a crocodilian needs to do after taking the first bite is to shake the prey and the meat tears apart as easily as the perforated paper in your notebook. But a crocodilian's jaws are a combination of astonishing strength and unbelievable weakness.

On the one hand, crocodilians can clamp their jaws in a bite strong enough to crush the legs of a cow. They have strong muscles controlling their upper jaws. A large crocodile's jaws can exert a crushing force of about 29,000 pounds! But crocodilians are too weak to open their jaws if any pressure is being exerted. Place a rubber band around the snout of a 6-foot-long alligator and the animal is helpless.

A predator needs more than just teeth and a strong bite, though. Crocodilians tend to hunt at night, and their eyes show it. Like other nocturnal hunters, their pupils are vertical slits, opening wider than round pupils would to allow more light to enter the eye. They also have a reflective layer, the *tapetum lucidum,* in the back of the eye that helps crocodilians see better in dim light conditions. Just like sharks and cats, the tapetum lucidum gives crocodilians eyes that glow in the dark. And also like sharks and cats, each crocodilian eye is protected by a nictitating membrane, a third eyelid through which the animal can see. And crocodilians can see color.

# ALLIGATORS

Crocodilians often hunt in muddy waters, where they have difficulty seeing. Fortunately for them, crocodilians have a highly developed sense of smell. And even though they have no visible outer ears, just slits that are right behind their eyes, the crocodilian's sense of hearing is extraordinary. A mother can hear her

## DID YOU KNOW?

A CROCODILIAN'S TEETH ARE REPLACED THROUGHOUT MOST OF ITS LIFE. OLD CROCODILIANS ARE OFTEN FOUND TOOTHLESS, HOWEVER.

ALTWATER CROCODILES ARE FOUND IN RIVERS AND SWAMPS NEAR THE SEA.

babies calling while they are still in their eggs! The nostrils and ear slits of crocodilians come equipped with moveable flaps that close against the water.

Crocodilians are not picky eaters. Although size determines what they hunt, crocodilians will eat anything that comes their way. And crocodilians are lazy hunters. Okay, lazy may not be the right word for them, but crocodilians generally hunt by lying around until something tasty wanders by. It's important, then, for crocodilians to be well camouflaged.

Being the large animals that they are, crocodilians are quite easy to see when they are out of the water. Although given the opportunity, crocodilians will hunt during the day, but most of their hunting takes place at night, under the cover of darkness.

Generally, crocodilians hunt while they're in the water.

All that can be seen of a crocodilian in the water are what appear to be three lumps: two eyes and the nostrils. The crocodilian's dark mottled coloring is enough to blend into the darkness of the water, but often its head is covered with algae and mud, further enhancing the camouflage effect.

So let's set the stage. It's dusk. The air is calm. Birds are singing. There's not a ripple in the water, which is flecked with algae and other aquatic plants. A herd of zebras stops at the water's edge to drink the life-giving liquid. Suddenly, screaming and commotion overtakes the herd. You take a closer look and see that something in the water seems to have taken hold of a zebra's nose. You can't believe your eyes because the zebra isn't resisting much and even seems to be walking willingly into the water. Soon, the zebra's nose is pulled underwater and the zebra drowns.

Again, suddenly, you see commotion in the water. It's a Nile crocodile spinning the now-dead zebra until parts of its body become detached. Then the crocodile takes a piece of meat in its jaws, raises its head, and swallows it whole. Chances are other crocodiles will come around to feast on this kill, since a zebra is much too large a prey for one crocodile's meal.

That's just one way crocodilians catch their prey. A crocodilian spotting a bird roosting in nearby trees can leap 5 feet into the air without warning, snatching up the hapless bird in its deadly jaws. And from its underwater camouflage, a crocodilian can launch itself out of the water onto the bank with surprising speed, and even run up the bank to snatch unsuspecting prey.

Underwater, a crocodilian captures prey by keeping its mouth open and swinging its head sideways, either trapping fish or just sweeping the fish into its jaws. Crocodilians have a flap at the back of their throats that closes to keep them from swallowing a lot of water. Crocodilians will use this sideways head swing on land to knock prey senseless before the kill.

Crocodilians can't move their jaws from side to side—in other words, they can't chew. Instead, they point their noses to the sky and rely on gravity to help them swallow meat whole. That's why crocodilians have to break apart their larger prey before eating.

When people are attacked by crocodilians, it's because they look like easy prey. In areas where most crocodilian attacks are recorded, people spend a lot of time on shorelines and even in the water. In Africa, Asia, and Australia, many people still bathe and wash their clothes in crocodile-infested waters. In the United States, tourists come to see wildlife in the unique environment of the Florida Everglades, where alligators make their home. In many cases, warning signs are posted and sometimes ignored by people. But despite the dangers some crocodilians pose to people and other animals, some species do a lot to help the environment and keep the local wildlife alive.

**DID YOU KNOW?**

**THE TEMPERATURE OF THE NEST DETERMINES WHETHER THE BABY ALLIGATORS DEVELOPING IN THE EGGS WILL BE MALES OR FEMALES**

# CHAPTER FOUR

# Crocodilians as Environmentalists

Crocodilians spend much of their time in the water. But they have to start their lives on dry ground. For example, when a female American alligator is ready to lay eggs, she gathers mud and plants to build nests that are up to 3 feet high. These nests are built on or near a body of water. In wetlands, alligator nests are often the highest and driest spots around. This is good news for other reptiles.

Alligators use their nests to lay and incubate their own eggs, of course. But their nests help out other animals as well. Other reptiles may lie on an alligator's nest, basking in the sun, and some turtles, snakes, and lizards lay their eggs in alligator nests. Animals such as raccoons raid alligator nests for their tasty eggs.

Female alligators defend their nests, some more rigorously than others. But typically if a person threatens a nest, the alligator rushes over to the intruder with her mouth open wide, hissing her warning. Most of her aggression toward intruders is all bluff, but I wouldn't want to test a female alligator guarding a nest, would you?

Some alligators spend their whole lives in one body of water. The water never dries out and food is plentiful. But some areas have wet and dry seasons. During the wet season, alligators may wander from this marsh to that pond, checking out different areas for the best food. But then there is the dry season.

## DID YOU KNOW?

A FEMALE ALLIGATOR MAY
BRING HER YOUNG TO A GATOR HOLE TO
WATCH OVER THEM AND KEEP THEM SAFE
FROM ENEMIES SUCH AS SNAKES, RACCOONS,
AND BLACK BEARS.

## Gator Holes

When bodies of water dry up, alligators come to the rescue. They use their bodies, including their heads, to scoop out the earth. They expose water that is just below the surface to make a pond about 10 feet across. These are called gator (short for alligator) holes. But there's more. Alligators dig a tunnel, again about 10 feet long or longer, that ends in a sort of den. The tunnel stays filled with water even if the pond above dries up. The den is filled with air.

In times of drought, gator holes are lifesavers. As you may have guessed, gator holes bring water to plants and other animals. Plants thrive and are food for some animals; fish and other aquatic life seek refuge in these temporary ponds; and water birds find their meals in these areas of flourishing wildlife. The alligator wins and so does its neighbors. So now that we've seen how crocodilians can help the environment, let's take a look at ways we humans have found to use crocodilians.

# Crocodilians as Big Business

Wherever crocodilians and people share land, people have been able to make use of crocodilians. Crocodilians have been eaten, and the scales from their ridged backs have been made into perfume and medicine along with their internal organs. Their teeth and feet have been made into necklaces and key chains, and of course, their skins have been made into expensive leather handbags, wallets, shoes, and belts. As a matter of fact, crocodilians have been hunted so extensively that many species have been hunted almost to extinction.

For example, American alligators were so abundant in the southeastern United States in the late 1700s that people marveled over their numbers. People realized that alligator hides make wonderful products, and in the 1800s about 3 million alligators were killed in Florida. That doesn't include the numbers killed in other states. In 1961, so few alligators existed in Florida that alligator hunting was banned. By 1972, if you killed an alligator in Florida, you would have been fined $5,000!

Fortunately, alligator populations were still strong in remote swamps that hunters couldn't reach. With this breeding population still intact and with protection from the government, alligators have made a tremendous comeback. They are so plentiful that they are used to make all sorts of leather goods once again. Now, many alligators are raised on alligator farms, and some of these farms are open to tourists.

Crocodilians have survived millions of years on earth. They have been worshiped and feared and have provided us with food, medicine, magic, and leather goods. As with all predators, we must respect the crocodilian's deadly power and take responsibility for staying out of reach of its killer jaws. And as with all predators, even the deadliest, crocodilians are important to the health of our environment, and they are an integral part of the web of life.

# Index

# INDEX

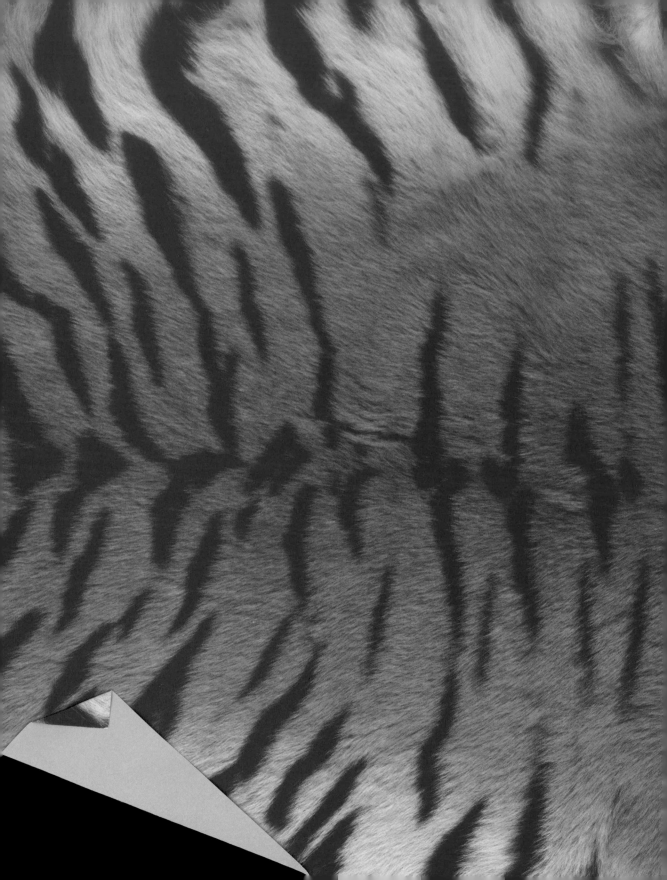